THE MINI STORY

THE **MINI** STORY

GILES CHAPMAN

The
History
Press

Published in the United Kingdom in 2011 by
The History Press
The Mill · Brimscombe Port ·
Stroud · Gloucestershire · GL5 2QG
www.thehistorypress.co.uk

Reprinted 2014, 2019

British Library Cataloguing in Publication Data
A catalogue record for this book is available from the
British Library.

ISBN 978-0-7524-6282-0

▶ *The last Classic Mini
from 2000 with the first
Morris Mini of 1959.*

*Title page: The Russ Swift
Mini Display Team in
action!*

Typesetting and origination by The History Press
Printed in China

CONTENTS

The Mini revolutionised the layout of the compact car. It opened new frontiers in passenger accommodation, driver pleasure and owner economy, while its shortcomings never elicited more than passing gripes. The Mini brought engineering excellence and egalitarian style to everyone, and then changed the face of motorsport forever.

Today, we live in fickle times when a mainstream family car appears obsolete if it's been in showrooms for five years. Yet the Mini was on sale for an extraordinary 41 years, during which time its pioneering design remained unchanged from the day in 1959 when it was revealed to a disbelieving world.

Did You Know?

In 1967, a bunch of students decided to see how many of them could squeeze inside a Mini. The uncomfortable answer was 24. The record was upped to 26 in 1986 in a Noel Edmonds TV stunt.

A motoring phenomenon, then; one made all the more remarkable by being the vision of a single individual – Alec Issigonis. The only son of an Anglo-Greek father and a German mother, Alexander Arnold Constantine Issigonis was born in 1906 in the Turkish town of Izmir (then called Smyrna). His engineer dad died when Alec was 16, and he and his mother settled in England. Two years later, he took to the road in a small Singer car, driving his mother all over Europe in it and learning, en route, how to keep it running. This experience helped steer him towards a three-year mechanical engineering course at London's Battersea Polytechnic.

As he wasn't too keen on maths, progress through academe was mediocre. Yet he showed intuitive design brilliance in preparing and racing an Austin Seven and,

later on, building his own single-seater racing car stuffed with clever technical solutions and ingenious ways to minimise weight. These skills secured him a job at Coventry carmaker Humber, where he was assigned in 1934 to work on independent front suspension systems. Two years later, he was poached by Morris, based in Oxford, to perform similar duties.

In the turmoil of the Second World War, Issigonis's can-do attitude served him well, and by 1941 he was chief engineer and leading a team planning (when time away from war work allowed) Morris's all-new family car under the codename 'Mosquito'. When it was launched as the Morris Minor in 1948 it was an instant hit, and showed the full scope of Alec Issigonis's capabilities, from its neat packaging and mechanical simplicity to the sheer unalloyed pleasure

Sir Alec Issigonis, without whose genius the Mini wouldn't have happened.

of a car with well sorted steering and roadholding.

The Minor would become, in 1959, the first British car to top one million sales.

Meanwhile, though, in 1952 Morris and arch-rival Austin merged to form the British Motor Corporation. The omens were not good for Issigonis. The influence in the merger was skewed towards Austin and he felt his power base was diminishing. Issigonis had grown accustomed to getting his own way – doing things by his preferred methods or not at all. A passionate and inspired lateral thinker, once he'd garnered his reputation for being 'right' about stuff, it often took just a thumbnail sketch and a persuasive argument to bedazzle people into backing his proposals. That wasn't going to be so easy at BMC, so he opted to leave and join Alvis, where he was given free rein to create an all-new V8 luxury car.

The grass there turned out to be greener but no more gratifying. Three years of

arduous work was rendered pointless when Alvis changed strategy and abruptly cancelled Issigonis's project. A career crisis seemed inevitable, but a rapprochement with Austin saved the day. They needed him back at Longbridge where there was a distinct torpor in 'The Kremlin', the administration block where new models were created.

The Minor and Austin A30 economy cars had been consistently popular but other, larger Austin models struggled to tempt customers away from, in particular, Ford's Consul and Zephyr. BMC chief Sir Leonard Lord made overtures to Issigonis, and he returned to the company in 1955 as deputy technical director . . . with the proviso that he had a free hand to oversee engineering programmes. The Minor, after all, had confounded its critics, so there was every

◀ A BMW Isetta in Gibraltar in 1959 – the sort of bubble car the Mini was gunning for.

9

Issigonis's now-famous sketch of 1958, showing how and why the Mini would make sense.

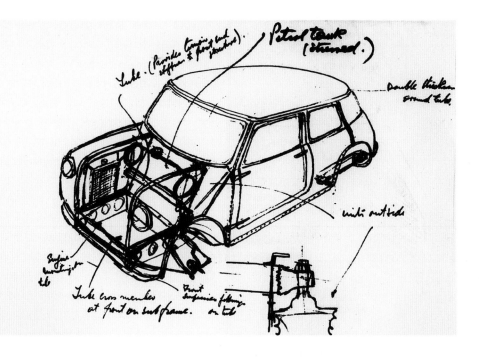

Did You Know?
Issigonis is said to have got the idea for using roller welders, to produce the Mini's characteristic exterior seams, after watching a Morris Minor fuel tank being made.

reason to believe Issigonis could spin his magic again.

The 1956 fuel crisis resulting from Egyptian president Nasser's seizure of the Suez Canal then became the catalyst for the Mini. Public alarm over petrol rationing was countered by an armada of appalling, hastily designed three-wheelers and 'bubble cars'. Lord thought his company should offer a better alternative – a real car, but in miniature – and he instructed Issigonis to funnel all his efforts into creating one. Aged 51 and familiar to colleagues as a pedant and a tinkerer, his enthusiasm for this task proved boundless. On paper napkins over lunch or in the little drawing pad he carried, he sketched and calculated constantly, consigning ideas to paper the moment they occurred to him. His team struggled to keep pace with his restless mental energy.

By early 1957, he'd drawn up his highly ingenious concept for 'ADO 15' (the project's Austin Drawing Office codename) containing several leaps of engineering imagination. The new car would be smaller than anything BMC had built before, but still offer space for four adults and their luggage. 80 per cent of its 'footprint' would be devoted to passengers and cargo. Therefore, the car's 'package' got his overriding attention. As it was to be just 10ft in total length, boot capacity would be limited, so Issigonis planned to utilise any spare spaces inside for accommodating cargo.

The car might have been shorter still. Late on in the design work, Issigonis had staff slice a design model in half and

The front-wheel drive 'powerpack' was cradled in a modular subframe.

then inch the two ends apart until he finally cried 'Stop!' at 120in. All this meant minimising the intrusion the car's drivetrain elements made on the passenger cabin, setting Issigonis on the miniaturisation trail. Front-wheel drive ensured the entire powerpack was unified in one place. The BMC A-Series engine – the only item Lord insisted be carried over – was mounted transversely across the front of the car, with the four-speed gearbox tucked underneath it, actually inside the engine's oil sump. The radiator was placed at the side of the engine bay.

Along with the steering and front suspension, this lot was cradled in a subframe bolted to the Mini's monocoque structure. Another subframe at the back held the rear wheels and suspension. Hard to believe today when you drive an original Mini but this did actually eliminate much of the vibration that would otherwise have arisen, as well as reducing stress on the structure, while the modular construction system meant it would be easy to develop Mini derivatives.

Power was transmitted to the front wheels via novel, Issigonis-created constant-velocity joints. They consisted of a ball bearing surrounded by three cages, two of which were connected, respectively, with the incoming and outgoing driveshafts. This, in turn, allowed a sufficient steering angle without distortion or undue articulation, minimising kickback in the steering . . . and endowing the little car with go-kart-like responses!

Did You Know?
More SU carburettors, made in Erdington, Birmingham, have been fitted to Minis than any other car – 5.5m in total.

Early running prototypes had a traditional Austin grille that lifted with the bonnet.

The basic shape is established but much detail changed from this 1957 styling proposal.

The suspension itself was primarily space-saving, but also highly effective. It was perfected by consultant engineer Dr Alex Moulton using two compact cones with a layer of rubber in between instead of the usual coil, torsion or leaf springs. The upper cone was bolted firmly to the subframe, the lower rested on the wheel mount. As the rubber hardened under increasing pressure, this gave the classic Mini a progressive suspension set-up. It was so good at soaking up knocks that only small telescopic dampers – shock absorbers – were needed; they were fastened outside on upper front wishbones and rear longitudinal control arms for a smooth response to sudden pressures.

The car's wheels were positioned at its extreme corners. Their unusually small diameter was to fit compact wheelarches

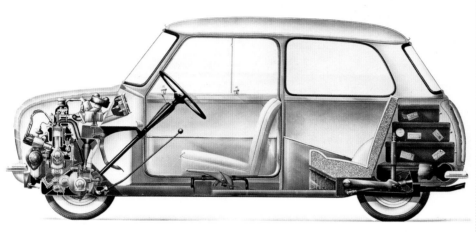

◄ *This ghosted side elevation clearly shows the Mini's superb packaging.*

Did You Know?
Alec Issigonis designed the door bins in early Minis around full-size gin bottles – essential for his favourite tipple of a dry Martini.

that wouldn't steal volume from the interior. Legend has it that Alec Issigonis said to Tom French, Dunlop's chief designer, 'Give me wheels *this* size.' Mr French measured the space between Issigonis's outstretched hands with a ruler. It was 10 inches. Whether true or not, Dunlop went on to make these specially sized wheels and tyres as part of Issigonis's exacting requirements.

There were sliding windows in the two doors. They were cheap to manufacture and the space in the doorframes they

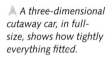 *A three-dimensional cutaway car, in full-size, shows how tightly everything fitted.*

No nook or cranny was too small to be useful for storing small items.

The incredible thing is, most of this lot would fit inside the 1959 Austin Se7en.

freed up was given over to deep storage bins for maps or handbags, moulded into the trim panels. A similar desire to open up storage space underscored Issigonis's minimalist instrumentation in the form of one large, single, circular dial combining speedo, fuel gauge and warning lights for oil pressure, battery and headlamp full-on beams. Rather than being embedded in a dashboard, this sat in the centre of a full-width shelf, the space either side available for in-car clobber like hats, gloves, parcels

Did You Know?
At one time, planners within the British Motor Corporation were going to call their new baby car the Austin Newmarket, to put it into line with the Cambridge and Westminster models.

and books. Below this were just about the only switches the driver needed, two toggles to activate the windscreen wipers and the lights.

The car was instantly redolent of Issigonis's clever thinking. It also reflected his personal idiosyncrasies. As a chain-smoker, he made sure it had an ashtray. But he hated listening to the radio when he drove, so there was nowhere to install one. The separate starter button had almost died out on mainstream cars by the late 1950s, yet Issigonis insisted one be fitted. It jutted from the front footwell behind the gearlever, had its own shroud so it couldn't be pressed accidentally . . . and would be quickly dropped.

It was an incredible feat to turn all this clever thinking into a working prototype in just seven months, but Issigonis made

it happen. He invited the boss, Leonard Lord, to come for a spin around the factory grounds.

'We drove round the Plant, and I was really going like hell,' Issigonis recalled later. 'I'm certain he was scared, but he was very impressed by the car's roadholding – something that could never be said of other economy cars of the era. So when we stopped outside his office, he got out and simply said, "All right, build this car."'

Apart from the drivetrain itself, the other factor giving the Mini its great handling was its torsional strength. The bare bodyshell weighed just 309lb but its exceptional stiffness was provided by two sills extending from front to rear, a lightweight tunnel in the middle of the car housing the exhaust system, and the wheelarches. Crosswise, the robust bulkhead between

A proud Alec Issigonis pictured on the day in 1959 when his baby was revealed to the media.

engine compartment and passenger cell, a strong crossmember beneath the front seats, and the rear bulkhead leading to the luggage compartment all contributed and, hence, permitted thin roof pillars and large windows to make the Mini light and airy.

Prototypes were also rapid – a little too much so. The engine, a four-cylinder, three-bearing crankshaft, overhead-valve unit, was the 948cc A-Series used in the Morris Minor 1000. It produced 37bhp at 5500rpm, which gave the lightweight,

FACTS & DATA: AUSTIN SE7EN (RENAMED AUSTIN MINI FROM 1962) AND MORRIS MINI-MINOR

On sale: 1959–64

Engine capacity: 848cc

Engine bore/stroke: 62.94/68.26mm

Engine power output: 34bhp at 5,500rpm

Fuel system: single-carburettor

Bodystyles: two-door, four-seater saloon; two-door, four-seater estate

Wheelbase: 80.2in (2,036mm); estate: 84.25in (2,140mm)

Length: 120.25in (3,054mm); estate: 129.9in (3,299mm)

Width: 55in (1,397mm)

Height: 53in (1,346mm); estate: 53.5in (1,360mm)

Luggage capacity: 5.5cu ft (155 litres); estate: 18.5-35.3cu ft
   (523–999 litres)

Top speed: 75mph; estate: 69mph

Acceleration, 0–60mph: 29.7sec; estate: 33.8sec

Fuel consumption, average: 40mpg; estate: 38mpg

Price when new: £496 standard and £537 De Luxe; estate: £623

The new AUSTIN SE7EN

⚠ *It may have been roomy but artistic licence was still taken to show just how spacious in advertising!*

1323lb car too much power for its brakes and suspension to rein in – and a 93mph top speed. It was decided instead to go for a smaller capacity, 848cc, giving a more modest 34bhp.

Changes made during 1958 included refining the body shape, particularly at the front where a traditional upright Austin grille like the A35's was swapped for a low, wide intake. Other aspects of the design aimed to reduce manufacturing costs, such as the rudimentary exterior door hinges, and a simple cord to slam the door shut rather than a handle (basic lever-operated handles would come with the De Luxe specification).

On 26 August 1959, the car was unveiled for the public, badged as Austin Se7en (a gimmicky way of linking it to the Austin Seven in the popular imagination) or Morris Mini-Minor 850 (ditto, Morris Minor, but much smarter thinking) to suit BMC's two sales networks. Wholly radical in concept and manufacture, the Mini made it from first sketch to metal reality in just over three years. The very first example built had been an Austin Se7en that rolled off the Longbridge production line on 4 April 1959. Then, five weeks later, on 8 May the first Morris Mini-Minor left Morris's Cowley factory in Oxford. The two were identical apart from their radiator grilles, hubcaps, badges and body paint colour: the Austin Se7en was available in Tartan red, Speedwell blue or Farina grey while the Morris Mini-Minor came in Cherry red, Clipper blue or Old English white.

Mini vans arrived in 1960 – these Austins are on the RAC's fleet – and had a ¼-ton payload.

A Mini presentation with your local Austin or Morris salesman was to marvel at the first car of a brand new age, and also to discover some of its finer points. The bottom-hinged boot lid, for instance, formed a drop-down luggage platform on to which larger items could be strapped. This compensated for the boot space lost to the spare wheel and battery, while the number plate on early cars was hinged to hang downwards so it was visible when transporting bulky loads.

The public was gobsmacked. It was unique. True, other new models vied for attention, especially the Triumph Herald and Ford Anglia 105E with their conventional layouts but slick, sharp-edged styling. But what *did* snag popular attention was the Mini's fantastically low price of £496. It appeared an unbelievable bargain; rivals were stunned. Ford, with its Merseyside-built Anglia just out at £589 and the Cortina development project in full swing, was particularly anxious to understand how BMC had achieved such value. It bought one of the earliest Minis and took it back to its Dagenham headquarters, where experts in product planning and component-buying

◀ *The Austin Se7en Countryman benefited from the Mini van's double rear doors.*

Did You Know?
The Mini inspired two memorable bumper stickers in the 1960s. One read 'SHORT VEHICLE', and the other 'You've just been Mini'd'.

carefully took apart its 3,016 individual pieces with forensic care. In doing so, they uncovered the Mini's Achilles' heel: its list price was about £30 less than it cost BMC to manufacture the car. The price had been set unrealistically low to win over otherwise

A Morris Mini-Traveller in Switzerland; the wood was axed for export sales.

sceptical customers but, essentially, the more Minis were sold the more money the company would lose!

This would be a fundamental problem with the car; some sources claim it didn't turn a healthy profit until the early to mid-

1980s, by which time BMC's successor company British Leyland had become one of the biggest bankrupts in British industrial history. No doubt about it, the Mini prematurely aged plenty of accountants within BMC and British Leyland. For sure, at the start, it was as time-consuming and complex as most other cars to assemble. It would have been even more so without another of Issigonis's deft touches. To utilise every spare inch of interior space, he put the car's body panel manual weld joins on the outside, giving the Mini its characteristic network of exterior 'seams'. Yet this feature proved resistant to change as the years rolled by. The production process of other cars was refined and streamlined, but the Mini remained as labour-intensive to build as it was at the start, stubbornly untouched by assembly line robots.

Consumer wariness meant that, in 1960, only 116,000 Minis were sold – way below BMC's capacity. This was despite a rapturous reception in the specialist press, typified by this from *The Autocar* in 1959, 'Throwing convention to the winds often produces freaks in the automotive world, but when done by a clever and imaginative designer the result may be outstanding. This is certainly the case with the Morris Mini-Minor.'

The catalyst for the Mini's sudden popularity – with fuel supply concerns and economic deprivation receding as the 1960s got into its stride – was simple word-of-mouth about what it was like to drive. Owners soon discovered it offered something no economy car had ever possessed before: sheer driving exhilaration. With that rubber springing

Did You Know?
At Longbridge in 1959, each Mini took two hours to assemble on a moving production line 220 yards long. A 10-hour night shift would see 220 cars completed.

and those thin seats, the ride could always be jarring, but the car's roadholding and handling was an absolute revelation. The surefootedness of front-wheel drive and the racing car-like sensation of having a wheel at each corner endowed the Mini with astounding nimbleness and corner-taking ability. This made it extremely swift from A to B; so the meagre power from its 848cc engine mattered little, while its fuel economy was a valuable bonus.

New model activity, meanwhile, was intensive almost immediately. First off the block, in May 1960, was a tiny Mini van with steel side panels and double doors at the back. The wheelbase was extended by 3in and the overall length by 10in, and there were both Austin and Morris editions. Four months later, the Austin Se7en Countryman and Morris Mini-Minor Traveller made their debut – two pint-size estate cars using the van structure and rear doors but with sliding side windows and a rear seat that folded flat into the floor to swallow 35cu ft of luggage. For a family resemblance to the Morris Minor Traveller, the rear body section featured a varnished wood frame although, unlike on the Minor where was this structural, the Mini's wood sections were glued on for that 'half-timbered' effect.

The following year, Austin and Morris pick-ups arrived. Featuring a drop-down tailgate, these could carry a quarter of a ton of cargo, just like the vans. And then in September the Riley Elf and Wolseley Hornet twins were launched. Resplendent in their luxury marque liveries, including upright traditional front grilles and boasting smartly-trimmed interiors with part-leather

The useful Mini pick-up was another long-wheelbase debutante of 1961.

covered seats, they were much more practical than the standard Minis because of the boxy extended boot at the back with its enlarged capacity. Bracketing the boot lid were tiny rear fins that echoed the style of BMC's larger cars, while the Riley

Luxury was added to the Mini's attributes in the 1961 Wolseley Hornet, and the similar Riley Elf.

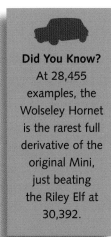

Did You Know?
At 28,455 examples, the Wolseley Hornet is the rarest full derivative of the original Mini, just beating the Riley Elf at 30,392.

32

also included a full-width wood veneer dashboard. Both offered an attractive package although, curiously, they were for years rather mocked by diehard Mini fanatics.

Alec Issigonis's strategy was proving sound. In recognition of his talents, in 1961 he joined the board of the Austin Motor Company as technical director, two years later joining the main BMC board. With Mini sales burgeoning, he was now closely involved with bringing his Mini packaging discipline to bigger cars; the 1100/1300 of 1962 would be another rip-roaring success, although the 1800/2200 models of 1964 fared less well against conventional competition from Ford and Vauxhall.

Issigonis, though, found fame outside the industry – elevating car design to more of an art than a dreary engineering discipline. He became good pals with Lord Snowdon, the photographer husband of Princess Margaret and an avid Mini owner and evangelist. Snowdon knew his sister-in-law – the queen – was a keen driver, and arranged for Issigonis to give her a demonstration drive in a new Mini in Windsor Great Park in 1960. Protocol forbade any relaying of her reaction, of course, but the overall royal 'blessing' marked the Mini's rapid accession to London society, where it became an instant 'It Car'. And then the little brick was adopted by 'names' – pop stars, TV celebrities, film actors and politicians. Customers stampeded into dealers, and the orders poured in.

ssigonis generally disdained suggestions that his thrifty runabout could manage more power. That is, until his long-time friend John Cooper, top Formula 1 car constructor, had sampled a Mini and realised that, with its incredible handling, it offered tremendous potential to shine in motorsport.

John Cooper, racing car tycoon, with his toddler son Mike and a mid-engined Cooper F1 car.

◀ *This Morris Mini-Cooper, with 55bhp-tuned engine, is photographed in 1964.*

272 PJO

This was before the basic Mini had even gone on sale but at the very time the Cooper Car Company was on top of its game in Formula 1; its trend-setting mid-engined racing cars were about to win the Constructor's World Championship and Driver's Championship (for the Australian Jack Brabham) in 1959, and then again in 1960.

Cooper's engineers set about tuning the engine, increasing capacity to 997cc by reducing the bore from 62.9 to 62.4mm and enlarging the stroke from 68.3 to 81.3mm. They raised the compression ratio from 8.3 to 9.0, incorporated larger intake valves and twin carburettors, increased the size of the exhaust bore and reinforced the crankcase so the engine could withstand the power hike from 34 to 55bhp. Transmission ratios were changed so the car could

accelerate faster in each gear, and the front wheels were equipped with tiny, 7in Lockheed disc brakes.

The first prototype, completed in 1959, hinted at the car's sparkling possibilities. John Cooper despatched F1 driver Roy Salvadori to the Monza test circuit in Italy in it for some sustained high-speed track-testing. He reached the destination an hour before his colleague Reg Parnell . . . who was driving an Aston Martin DB4. The following year, 12 works and privately-entered standard Minis tackled the Monte Carlo Rally, and showed enormous promise while not featuring among the winners – the highest placing was 23rd overall for privateers Riley and Jones.

FACTS & DATA: AUSTIN SE7EN COOPER (RENAMED AUSTIN COOPER FROM 1962) AND MORRIS MINI-COOPER

On sale: 1961–4 in 997cc form, 1964–7 in 998cc form

Engine capacity: 997 and 998cc

Engine bore/stroke: 62.43/81.28mm (997cc), 64.6/76.2mm

Engine power output: 55bhp at 6000rpm (997cc) and 5,800rpm (998cc)

Fuel system: single-carburettor (997cc), twin-carburettor (998cc)

Bodystyle: two-door, four-seater saloon

Wheelbase: 80in (2,0032mm)

Length: 120.25in (3,054mm)

Width: 55in (1,397mm)

Height: 53in (1,346mm)

Luggage capacity: 5.5cu ft (155 litres)

Top speed: 87mph (997cc), 90mph (998cc)

Acceleration, 0–60mph: 18sec (997cc), 16.8sec (998cc)

Fuel consumption, average: 27mpg (997cc), 30mpg (998cc)

Price when new: £679

Three Mini Coopers in close-matched action during a saloon car race, Silverstone, 1965.

◀ In 1965, you could drive your roadgoing Cooper to a circuit, tape over the headlights, and join the grid!

Hopkirk and Liddon powering through a gravel stage on the 1964 Monte Carlo Rally.

The Cooper S's first Monte win came in 1964, when Paddy Hopkirk (left) drove to victory.

gave the go-ahead to build a series of 1,000 production 'Mini Coopers', making it eligible for production car events, and agreed to pay Cooper a royalty on each one. Introduced in September 1961, the showroom model was immediately identifiable by its wheels drilled for lightness and ventilation and its two-tone paintjob with a contrasting-colour roof panel. It was a profitable sell-out at £679, and all thoughts about it being a limited edition were quickly forgotten.

None of the three BMC works Mini entries in 1961 finished. But then, after the Cooper transformation, the car's luck changed dramatically. In 1962, it saw its first outright international rally victory as Pat Moss (Stirling Moss's sister) drove a Mini Cooper to win the 1962 Tulip Rally in Holland.

There was a special car here waiting to be unleashed, all evidence suggested. So BMC chief executive George Harriman

▶ *Timo Mäkinen and Paul Easter won the devilishly arctic 1965 Monte Carlo Rally.*

A Cooper S on the infamous 1966 Monte, where cars were disqualified for non-compliant dipped-beam headlights.

Then Finland's Rauno Aaltonen was running second in the 1962 Monte when over-enthusiastic driving put his Cooper on its roof less than 2 miles from the finish, and it was all over; he was lucky to escape the ensuing fireball.

In 1963, Paddy Hopkirk's Cooper won the Tour de France, swiftly followed by a class victory for Aaltonen on the Monte, and third overall, plus second-in-class and sixth overall for Hopkirk.

The pace, and driver confidence in the cars, was hotting up. So was the plucky Mini Cooper itself. In late 1963, it was upgraded to become the Cooper S. Issigonis and Cooper collaborated on the engine, which was bored out to 1071cc to keep it below the 1100cc level to qualify for the intended motorsport classes. With maximum revs of 7,200rpm, it was a little screamer, with peak power of 70bhp at 6,200rpm. This guaranteed greased-lightning acceleration of 0–62mph in 13 seconds, and top speed was upped from 84mph to over 90. Brake diameter increased by half-an-inch and a servo was fitted to keep the tiny terror in check.

In January 1964, Hopkirk and co-driver Henry Liddon finally took their Cooper S registration number 33 EJB to an outright victory in the Monte Carlo Rally, trouncing factory teams from Citroën, Mercedes-Benz and especially the thunderous Ford Falcon squad. Timo Mäkinen's Cooper S was fourth, Rauno Aaltonen's sixth.

Mäkinen and co-driver Paul Easter would swipe another Monte Carlo win in 1965 in one of the new 76bhp, 1275cc Cooper S cars, registered AJB 44B, an epic drive underscored by the fact the duo incurred not one penalty point despite some of

◄ Aaltonen and Liddon on the 1967 Monte, where victory made it a Mini hat-trick.

A Morris Mini-Minor making light of London traffic in 1963; note the script on the bus and the van.

the snowiest conditions ever seen on the thousands of miles of the event. Only 35 of the 237 cars entered made the finish, three of them Mini Cooper Ss.

Mäkinen was set to make it a Cooper S hat-trick in 1966, but his 'winning' car GRX 555D was disqualified (along with Aaltonen's second-placed car, Hopkirk's in third, and a Lotus Cortina in fourth position) for headlights whose dipped beam failed regulations. The questionable victory was handed to a Citroën. But the 'three musketeers' were back undaunted in 1967, and dominated the show in style. LBL 6D, driven by Aaltonen/Liddon won the rally to tumultuous applause from spectators; Hopkirk came home sixth and Mäkinen forty-first.

Aaltonen took third, Tony Fall fourth and Hopkirk fifth in the Monte in 1968 but, after then, there was nothing more to prove. Stuart Turner, BMC competitions manager from 1961 to 1967, later recalled it was the 'right car at the right time'; the Mini's showing confirmed it as among the most significant rally cars ever.

The Cooper S also made an epic showing in British Saloon Car Championships driven by the likes of John Rhodes, Sir John Whitmore, John Fitzpatrick and Alec Poole, and a host of other motorsport branches to boot. Indeed, dozens of outstanding motorsport careers began behind the wheel of a Mini, including those of future Formula 1 World Champions Graham Hill, Jackie Stewart, John Surtees, Jochen Rindt and James Hunt. Triple Championship winner Niki Lauda was another, the young Austrian entering a Mini in his first hillclimb in Linz in April

Hopkirk and Crellin came fifth in the 1968 Monte; similar roof racks became must-have items in 1990s Japan for Mini owners.

1968 in which he came an immediate second; within three weeks he was tasting racing victory.

The 'halo' effect on all Minis of its widespread motorsport success was manifest not just in rising sales, but also in a vast 'aftermarket' in dedicated accessories, tuning parts and customising services so that each Mini could be personalised around its driver's aspirations. Performance-minded owners could soon choose from a bewildering array of bolt-on products to soup up their own Minis for road or track, including from 1964 an 'official' range of go-faster goodies from BMC's Special Tuning division. These included competition camshafts, bigger carburettors, alternative gear sets, and those distinctive Minilite magnesium-alloy spoked wheels.

Still others preferred to go the pint-sized limousine route. The concept was originated by London coachbuilder Harold Radford in response to his customers' requests for a city runabout to match their Rolls-Royces and Bentleys, and launched in 1963 as the Mini De Ville in full-spec Grande Luxe form at £1,080, or the slightly cheaper Bel Air.

Although every car was slightly different, typical upgrades included fat wheels, blacked-out windows, full leather interiors, walnut dashboards, gleaming two-tone paintjobs, full-length sunroofs, elaborate hi-fis and cocktail cabinets, and a galaxy of electrical extras from aerials to window lifts. Some were given hatchback rear doors with a split/folding rear seat, restyled fronts incorporating stacked headlight clusters from Mercedes-Benzes, or even (no, really!)

worked over so the weld seams were turned inwards and covered over for a smooth overall look. It proved such a lucrative business that other firms quickly joined in, including Hooper & Co. and Wood & Pickett.

Celebrities from ballet legend Margot Fonteyn and heart-throb Steve McQueen to Beatles Paul McCartney and Ringo Starr owned such cars, but few were as fixated on special Minis as the actor Peter Sellers. He had several adorned with basketweave wickerwork panels on the outside, among other embellishments, and his own Radford Mini De Ville featured heavily in his 1964 Pink Panther comedy film *A Shot In The Dark*. But even ordinary Minis were part of the 'scene' for the stars of the 1960s. Beatle John Lennon bought one in 1964 even though he didn't have a driving licence; George Harrison lent his Mini to Eric Clapton in 1967 and only got it back three years later. Meanwhile, Spencer Davis wrote the biggest hit his band ever had while driving through the night in the rainy Scottish Highlands on an almost empty tank. Nervously eyeing the fuel gauge gave him the title – 'Keep on Running' – that made the Spencer Davis Group a household name.

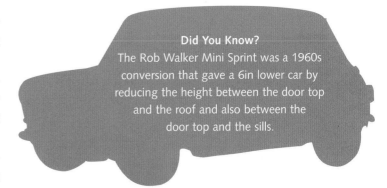

Did You Know?
The Rob Walker Mini Sprint was a 1960s conversion that gave a 6in lower car by reducing the height between the door top and the roof and also between the door top and the sills.

MOKES, MARKS AND ITALIAN JOBS

The Moke in 1965 in what became its natural habitat – sun-kissed holiday resorts.

This is the prototype Mini Moke, which failed to win military hearts and minds.

Yet another decidedly hip Mini was the Moke, an open four-seater originally envisaged as a lightweight troop carrier. The 'buckboard' body shell was made up of the Mini floorpan with wide, box-shaped side-sills, together with a simple steel box to house the engine and support a windscreen. The Moke was meant to be parachuted into combat situations, and then be light enough to be carried on the shoulders of four burly squaddies if driving conditions overwhelmed it. British Army chiefs put prototype Mokes on trial in 1960, but their reaction was lukewarm. Its low ground clearance, tiny 10in wheels and two-wheel drive hindered progress over anything much more arduous than wet grass.

The Royal Navy bought a handful but the Army stuck to Land Rovers. A dogged Issigonis built an experimental four-wheel drive 'Twini Moke', with two engines and two transmissions giving 87bhp of power at each end. It gave, by all accounts, some invincible, snow-scattering demonstrations but military chiefs again spurned the Moke, maybe slightly concerned by the Twini's complexity, including its two gearlevers.

for one simple reason: it wasn't actually a car. As the Moke came with just a driver's seat – and, indeed, just one windscreen wiper – HM Customs & Excise classified it as a commercial vehicle, on which no VAT was payable. It was extremely slow, barely capable of 65mph and taking almost 22 seconds to hit 60mph, and super-basic. There was just one colour option: dark green.

The cunning bit was that, once you'd bought your Moke, you could turn it into a car again by adding three optional passenger seats, an extra wiper and flimsy sidescreens. In fact, some 90 per cent of Mokes were exported and sold as beach cars and hotel taxis in hot countries – it was Britain's eccentric riposte to America's dune buggy. Most of the remainder stayed in 1960s London, where Afghan-coated hippies shivered at the wheel as they waited at

Still, BMC didn't want to waste it. So it went on sale in January 1964 as an Austin or Morris Mini Moke, with an open-sided canvas tilt/hood and storage lockers built into its sides. The price was just £405, undercutting every other four-wheeled car,

Notting Hill traffic lights. *Motoring Which?* summed up the experience by pointing out, 'Driving through the back streets of Kensington in pouring rain in the Moke must rate, as an activity, very low on anyone's fun index.' Mokes featured prominently in cult ATV series *The Prisoner*, and in the amazing underground scenes in the Bond movie *The Man With The Golden Gun*. By 1967, the VAT man twigged to the Moke's tax dodge and swiftly reclassified it as a car, raising the price by £78. UK sales collapsed and in October 1968, British manufacture ended after 14,518 had been built (all but 1,467 exported), and the entire Moke tooling shipped to Sydney, Australia. It was manufactured there and later in Portugal until 1994.

But enough of highly-strung, specialised and esoteric Minis – what about the ordinary cars that normal mortals bought and drove? In 1965, after six years on sale, Mini sales would reach the momentous 1 million milestone. But by then the little car had already seen some significant changes to its winning formula.

A right little flier: this is a Morris Mini-Cooper S in 1966. Looks innocuous enough . . .

The most radical was in its suspension when, in 1964, the rubber cones were replaced by a system called Hydrolastic. Shared with the Austin/Morris 1100, this was an interconnected system incorporating sprung displacer units, which used rubber

valves to push fluids between front and back wheels. It was inspired by Citroën's self-levelling systems, and was part of Issigonis's zeal to harness the latest technology to enhance comfort. Each wheel carried a cylinder about the size of a 1-litre oilcan

◀ The entire Mini MkII range as it stood in 1968, when British Leyland took control of its destiny.

containing the spring and damper in one unit, and using a frost-resistant water emulsion as the damper fluid. The hydraulic chambers on the front and rear wheel dampers were connected by pressure hoses on each side of the car. That meant that, whenever a front wheel hit a road bump, some front hydraulic fluid was forced into its rear counterpart, lifting up the body slightly also at the rear. And vice versa, of course.

Another benefit of Issigonis's ongoing quest for improvement was the availability of automatic transmission in 1965, a clever, compact design from AP that beat its few rivals in having four speeds over the conventional three. By then, too, some dashboard controls had been rearranged so that, finally, they were now all within reach of a driver wearing a seatbelt!

FACTS & DATA: AUSTIN AND MORRIS MINI-COOPER S

On sale: 1963–4

Engine capacity: 1071cc

Engine bore/stroke: 70.64/68.26mm

Engine power output: 70bhp at 6,200rpm

Fuel system: twin-carburettor

Bodystyle: two-door, four-seater saloon

Wheelbase: 80in (2,032mm)

Length: 120.25in (3,054mm)

Width: 55in (1,397mm)

Height: 53in (1,346mm)

Luggage capacity: 5.5cu ft (0.16cu m)

Top speed: 91mph

Acceleration, 0–60mph: 13.5sec

Fuel consumption, average: 29mpg

Price when new: £695

An Austin Mini 1000 MkII interior was more ergonomic than ever, if you can believe it.

A Mini, like this Morris Mini 1000 MkII seen in 1968, was the car to be seen in around London.

The base Cooper models dispensed with their custom-built 997cc engine, instead adopting a twin-carburettor edition of the 998cc motor now also found in the Riley Elf and Wolseley Hornet.

Three years later and the cars were officially relaunched as the 'MkII' range, with an enlarged rear window and light clusters, and a square-cut grille. Another change was much appreciated by city-dwelling Mini buyers: a turning circle cut from 32 to 28ft. The larger 998cc engine option was also offered in the standard-shape cars, with more torque – 38lb/ft, up from 32 – and 4bhp more power to take output to 38bhp.

Yet the MkII revisions seem mild compared to what came in 1969 and the MkIII range. The Mini was now part of British Leyland and came in for close scrutiny from all quarters of the conglomerate – the newly-ennobled Sir Alec Issigonis no longer had the final say. And, no doubt to his chagrin, the Hydrolastic suspension, which was expensive to manufacture and unpopular with owners because of maintenance costs, was ditched and the rubber cone system reinstated. The door bins were dropped so proper wind-up windows could be fitted and the unsightly door hinges could be internalised.

The old BMC custom of offering different liveries of Mini for Austin and Morris dealers ended. 'Mini' became a marque in itself. All Mini manufacture was now centralised on the Longbridge plant south of Birmingham; the Mini line was removed from Oxford's Cowley works after it had churned out 602,817 Morris Mini saloons (vans, pick-ups, estates and Mokes always

A Morris Mini-Cooper S MkII making London swing in 1968.

came from Longbridge only). The slow-selling Elf, Hornet and Moke were axed and an alternative, upmarket Clubman

FACTS & DATA: MINI 1275GT

On sale: 1969–80

Engine capacity: 1275cc

Engine bore/stroke: 70.64/81.33mm

Engine power output: 59bhp at 5,300rpm (54bhp
   from 1974)

Fuel system: single-carburettor

Bodystyle: two-door, four-seater saloon

Wheelbase: 80.2in (2,036mm)

Length: 124.6in (3,165mm)

Width: 55.in (1,410mm)

Height: 53in (1,346mm)

Luggage capacity: 5.5cu ft (155 litres); 4.1cu ft
   (116 litres) from 1974

Top speed: 86mph in 1969, rising to 90mph in
   1971 (86mph from 1974)

Acceleration, 0–60mph: 14.7sec dropping to
   13.3sec in 1971 (14.6sec from 1974)

Fuel consumption, average: 30–35mpg

Price when new: £834

saloon and estate – garlanded with fake wood panels – was introduced, with a more welcoming interior and a Ford Cortina-like, square nose treatment that increased overall length by 4.3in (11cm). All other dimensions were unchanged.

For nine years, the Mini Cooper had represented the ultimate in compact

A close-ratio gearbox, superb mid-range torque and limpet-like grip made an Austin Cooper S MkII an overtaker's dream. (Photo: Classic & Sports Car)

It's 1969 and the square-fronted Clubman series is launched, here with the 1275GT to the fore.

performance thrills. Now, for the first time, came a hot Mini without the aura of the Formula 1 connection. The 1275GT was based on the Clubman but with a single-carburettor 1275cc A-Series motor for sparkling response rather than raw power. It came with Rostyle wheels – fake alloys, basically – and later Dunlop Denovo run-flat wheels/tyres. Plus, something no standard Cooper had ever required before: go-faster stripes!

The Cooper S continued to be available in MkIII guise until 1971, when British Leyland decided to sever its royalty deal

with John Cooper. A golden era closed. Yet the car was at the height of its global fame, having been given a starring role in the much-loved Michael Caine heist comedy caper *The Italian Job* of 1969, where its exhilarating driving dynamics were on full display.

'*The Italian Job* would be the longest commercial for a car ever made,' said the producer Michael Deeley in his 2008 autobiography. Nevertheless, he found BMC/British Leyland had a strange apathy to the living legend in its care; the company only let him have six cars at 'cost', meaning the film's budget had to stretch to buying another thirty at retail prices.

'Many of those who worked on the picture felt BMC's attitude was a sad reflection of the British car industry's marketing skills,' recalled Deeley.

Driving a Mini Cooper into a moving coach was just one of the high points of The Italian Job.

Making The Italian Job *required 36 Cooper Ss, and none survived the ordeal.*

 Did You Know?
Fruit grower Outspan commissioned six Mini-powered 'Oranges' in
1973 – bodied in glassfibre on shortened Mini floorpans to resemble
giant citrus fruit. One survives in the National Motor Museum, Beaulieu.

◀ This 1976 Mini 1000, despite its many qualities, was not the best car for enjoying Britain's expanding motorway network in comfort.

◀◀ Sir Alec Issigonis retired in 1971; here he is with his progeny (right to left), Austins Mini, 1100 and 1800.

The launch of the Renault 5 in 1972, the world's first 'supermini', triggered the Mini's decline.

Then again, the Mini was a mainstay of British Leyland sales at a time when the the company offered such dire fare as the Austin Maxi and Morris Marina. Indeed, in 1971 Mini sales reached an all-time annual peak, at a whopping 318,475. This was just before the new breed of 'supermini'

arrived, economy cars that used the Mini's technical concept but added more space and the versatility of a hatchback tailgate and folding rear seats. The Renault 5 was the breakthrough car here, swiftly followed by the Volkswagen Polo and Fiat 127. Issigonis's own supermini, codenamed 9X,

◀◀ *The Ford Fiesta took its bow in 1976, and proceeded to decimate Mini sales.*

◀ *At last, the cavalry: the Metro arrived in 1980 to help the Mini in its fight against rivals.*

had been canned on cost grounds, and he retired in 1971 feeling understandably miffed. For if the Mini's 1970s days are defined by anything, then it is stagnation. It was a national treasure that, aside from a larger, 1098cc engine in the Clubman in 1975, was largely neglected. A year later, the excellent Ford Fiesta arrived and would proceed to gnaw away at Mini sales.

The feeble British Leyland response in 1976 was to launch the first Mini limited edition, the 1000 Special, with chrome door mirrors, a fancy paintjob and reclining seats. Behind the scenes, the Metro was taking shape amid near constant political turmoil, but buyers had to wait until late 1980 to finally get their hands on this all-British Fiesta rival.

In 1979, finally, came signs the Mini was receiving some attention. As well as a limited edition to celebrate the car's 21st birthday, there was a new budget model, the 848cc Mini City, and the following year came the 998cc, 40bhp Mini HL and the Clubman-style HL estate. In 1982, to suit the straitened economic times, a high-

In 1979, this chirpy special edition was launched to celebrate the Mini's 21st birthday.

The 850 City was super basic, and aimed to re-establish the Mini as a value leader in mid-1979.

geared 'E' engine extended fuel economy while the new Mayfair model offered velvety upholstery, headrests and optional wide alloy wheels.

Rather more radical change came in 1984 when the wheels were increased to 12in in diameter and front disc brakes standardised across the range.

△ *The four-millionth Mini was this 1275GT in 1972, here displayed by Ethel from the British Leyland typing pool. Possibly.*

In Italy, Minis were built by Innocenti, which also created its own version with a hatchback and Bertone styling, seen here on the right.

Did You Know?
Renowned Poole-based customiser Andy Saunders chopped almost 3ft of length out of a Mini in 1984 to create the Mini Ha-Ha, reckoned to be the shortest Mini in the world.

With the Mini sealed in its own technical timewarp, the marketing people at what had become Austin Rover were now tasked with stoking interest in the car. This they achieved with a constant parade of limited editions throughout the 1980s, many of them referencing the car's Britishness and age-related milestones. It certainly chewed up ideas, but the production line at Longbridge was kept humming.

ORIGINAL MINI SPECIAL EDITIONS FOR THE UK

Name	Date	Number made	Name	Date	Number made
1000 Special	1976	3,000	Studio 2	1990	2,000
1100 Special	1979	5,000	Cooper (intro edition)	1990	1,000
Sprite	1983	2,500	Neon	1991	1,500
25	1984	5,000	British Open Classic	1992	1,000
Ritz	1985	3,725	Italian Job	1992	1,750
Chelsea	1986	1,500	Rio	1993	750
Piccadilly	1986	2,500	Tahiti	1993	500
Park Lane	1987	1,500	35	1994	1,000
Advantage	1987	2,500	Cooper Monte Carlo	1994	200
Red Hot/Jet Black	1988	2,000	Sidewalk	1995	1,000
Designer (Quant)	1988	2,000	EquinoX	1996	750
Rose/Sky	1989	1,000	Cooper 35 LE	1996	200
Racing/Flame	1989	2,000	Paul Smith	1998	300
Thirty	1989	3,000	Cooper LE	1998	100
Racing Flame/Checkmate	1990	2,500	40	1999	250

▶ As creator of the mini skirt itself, Mary Quant was a natural to endorse the 1988 Mini Designer limited edition.

▶▶ Among a plethora of limited editions, fashion giant Paul Smith's was, naturally, one of the best turned-out.

Rowan Atkinson, as Mr Bean, is funny, but the Mini's stagnation in the 1970s was no laughing matter.

The 1982 Mayfair, with its opulent seating and tinted glass, was the most luxurious standard Mini to date.

An interesting new source of sales success was Japan. Austin Rover started selling the Mini there in 1985, and within five years annual sales rocketed from 1,500 to 11,000, with buyers spending an average of £500 on accessories like a replica of the roof-mounted spare-wheel rack fitted to the 1967/8 Monte Carlo Rally Mini Cooper S.

'We were fortunate that we surfed a wave of interest in imported cars at the time of Japan's "bubble economy",'

said David Blume, who ran Austin Rover Japan. 'For Japanese people who love cars, owning one is the fulfilment of a dream. And also, of course, in a crowded country like this, it still delivers its promise: it still gets four people – okay, not with much luggage – around the city, and then fits into the smallest of parking spaces. It's the Tamagotchi factor: being cute and physically small is the appeal.'

The five-millionth Mini was made in 1986; it is fantastic that Sir Alec Issigonis could witness that (he passed away in 1988). Then pressure and input from David Blume saw the resurrection of the Mini Cooper in 1990, which cashed in once again on the car's heroic sporting pedigree. Sales soared.

Unlike the limited editions, this one was more than just decals. Under the bonnet a

Austin Rover needed a celebrity to see the five millionth Mini off the line. They chose Noel Edmonds.

FACTS & DATA: MINI COOPER

On sale: 1990–2001

Engine capacity: 1275cc

Engine bore/stroke: 70.64/81.33mm

Engine power output: 61bhp at 5,550rpm
(63bhp from 1992)

Fuel system: single-carburettor from 1990–2,
fuel-injection from 1992–2001

Bodystyle: two-door, four-seater saloon

Wheelbase: 80.1in (2,035mm)

Length: 120.25in (3,054mm)

Width: 55.5n (1,410mm)

Height: 53.25in (1,353mm)

Luggage capacity: 4.1cu ft (116 litres)

Top speed: 87mph, rising to 92mph in 1992

Acceleration, 0–60mph: 12.2sec dropping to 9.8sec
in 1992

Fuel consumption, average: 40mpg

Price when new: £6,995

▲ *There was deep joy among Mini devotees when the 1275cc Cooper returned in 1990 (this is a 1992 fuel-injected car).*

◀ *Only in the 1990s did the Mini get its first proper badge, equipped with wings like all the best British classic car logos.*

with the 1.3-litre fuel injection catalyst engine already featured since October 1991 in the Mini Cooper and as of August 1994 also in the 53bhp Mini, thanks to growing requirements to cut exhaust emissions.

In 1991 came something not seen since the Moke of 1964: a new bodystyle. German Mini specialist LAMM Autohaus devised a 'cabriolet' convertible conversion,

◄ German specialist LAMM created this Cabriolet in 1991, and sold 75 examples through Rover dealers.

1275cc A Series engine returned, in feisty 61bhp tune, and Minilite-style alloy wheels were standard under widened wheelarches. Plus, it was fully endorsed by John Cooper Garages, and the great man himself.

The 1.0-litre nevertheless clung on until 1992, after which all models were equipped

Did You Know?
The various owners of the Mini trademark have been quick to stamp on automotive infringement. When a Danish electric three-wheeler called the Mini-el City went on sale in 1992, swift court action by Rover saw it renamed the City-el PCV.

The LAMM Cabriolet was adapted by Rover and Karmann into a factory-built car in 1993.

with an all-round body kit concealing the substantial strengthening installed in the sills to reinstate the rigidity lost by slicing the steel roof off. With the hood stacked up at the back when folded rather like a pram, it was perhaps not the most elegant car but the quality of the work was excellent. So good, in fact, that Rover Group decided to buy the project after LAMM had sold just 75 examples. German soft-top experts Karmann combed through the design to prepare it for general sale in 1993. Always quite costly at over £12,000, Rover still managed to sell 1,000 examples up to 1996.

In 1997, the Rover 100, as the Metro was by then known, was axed and, almost unbelievably, the original Mini would outlast it by another four years. When the final 'classic' Mini was built on 4 October 2000, the production total was just shy of 5.4 million. This made it easily the best-selling single British car ever.

MEASURING MINIS IN THE MILLIONS

20,000 – 1959, first year of manufacture.

1,000,000 – 1965, the year the 70mph speed limit arrived (top speed of an 848cc Mini anyway).

2,000,000 – 1969, as man walked on the Moon and Concorde made its maiden flight.

3,000,000 – 1972, the year the first supermini, the Renault 5, went on sale.

4,000,000 – 1976, when all Minis gained two column stalks, a heated rear window and hazard warning lights.

5,000,000 – 1986, the actual car being driven off the line by Noel Edmonds.

5,387,062 – 2000, last year of manufacture.

ENTER THE MINI

In 1994, the penultimate episode in the history of the company variously known as Austin, BMC, British Leyland, BL, Austin Rover and Rover Group began when BMW bought the company from interim owner British Aerospace. A year later it set about doing something successive custodians of the Mini had shrunk away from: designing an all-new Mini. With BMW's commitment and huge financial resources, Rover's engineers started to shape the car the British motor industry had craved for so long.

The first, tantalising evidence of this was revealed at the 1997 Frankfurt Motor Show with a concept study of a MINI (note the capitals) Cooper. It was very much a modern

The 1997 Mini range was revamped, with these super-wide alloy wheels and tyres now among options.

Did You Know?

Rover built two Mini 'concept' cars in 1997, the stripped-out Mini Hot Rod and the super-luxurious Mini Limo, to show the extremes of possible Mini personalisation; the Mini Limo was the first car to feature a MiniDisc hi-fi.

interpretation of the original, familiar in overall profile but bigger, wider, chunkier and with the emphasis on sporty fun rather than austerity-minded frugality. The wheel-at-each-corner stance was adhered to faithfully. There were predictable grumbles about the car being untrue to Issigonis's founding Mini principles, but the reaction was overwhelmingly positive. The designer leading Project MINI, Frank Stephenson, wanted to keep the whole *spirit* of the Mini alive, not its original, creaking carcass, so there was an exaggeration of design detail and an emphasis on fun, with the requirement to carry four people a given, rather than a boast.

The basic Mini continued as the 1.3i and later the Seven; it still made a nifty, thrifty city runabout.

For one thing, it was almost 2ft longer. As the overhangs were minimal, all the extra space went into the cockpit. For another, a contrasting-colour roof – an icon on the first Coopers – was integral to the look, with the darkened windows wrapping around the car like a band. Meanwhile, the shoulder line of the car was established at its round headlights, while the broad, hexagonal grille shape picked up on the form familiar on all original Minis since 1967. The upright rear light clusters and chrome surrounds immediately evoked the 1959 original.

Inside, the accommodation was almost like a 2+2, with the emphasis on the two front seats at the expense of the relatively tight rear ones, and a gigantic, circular 'speedo' dominating the middle of the dashboard and housing all the car's dials and gauges.

The corporate background to the original Mini had always been turbulent. As final prototypes of the all-new car were pounding the roads and proving grounds of the West Midlands in May 2000, the final bombshell landed. BMW was exiting Rover by selling off Land Rover to Ford and hoisting the 'for sale' sign over Longbridge and its volume carmaking business. However, *not* included was Mini, which BMW was splitting off and retaining, nor Rover's brand new engine plant at Hams Hall, Birmingham. In the weeks that followed, during which the controversial Phoenix Consortium took on Rover, work on an assembly building for the new Mini at Longbridge was halted.

For export markets, the Kensington edition bid a golden goodbye to what was now being called the 'original' Mini.

This is an example of the last series of Mini Coopers, photographed in 2000.

GB V206 LOE

The last few Coopers come off the line at Longbridge in 2000; within five years, the factory would be finished too.

Rover's Nick Stephenson (right) presents the very last Mini to Bob Dover of the British Motor Industry Heritage Trust, for safekeeping.

89

90

◁ In 1997, BMW unveiled this concept called ACV30 as a tribute to the Mini's Monte Carlo Rally domination three decades earlier.

◁◁ Rover's British development team initially thought cars like the 1996 Spiritual and Spiritual Too, concepts for economy models, pointed the way towards a new Mini.

Towards the end of 1997, pictures of BMW's finalised 'New Mini' prototype were released.

Although four years away from being launched, the 'New Mini' concept was an accurate pointer to the future.

▶ *Enormous speedo in the centre of the dashboard redolent of the 1959 Mini.*

▶▶ *'Clamshell' bonnet took wing tops and headlights with it as it swung open to reveal the 1.6-litre Tritec engine.*

The Rover 75 line was shifted from Cowley to Longbridge and BMW began the massive task of re-equipping (what they now called) Plant Oxford to build (what they now called) the MINI.

The car made its first official appearance in November 2000 at the Berlin Motor

Show, and finally entered showrooms a year later in base 90bhp MINI One and sporty 115bhp MINI Cooper guises. Under the bonnet, there was no trace of the faithful A-Series motor, nor Rover's well-respected all-aluminium K Series.

The customer-ready MINI Cooper of 2001, which fans were pleased to see had a wheel at each corner.

FACTS & DATA: MINI COOPER

On sale: 2001–6

Engine capacity: 1598cc

Engine bore/stroke: 77/85.5mm

Engine power output: 115bhp at 6,000rpm

Fuel system: fuel-injection

Bodystyle: three-door, four-seater saloon

Wheelbase: 2,467mm (97.1in)

Length: 3,655mm (143.9in)

Width: 1,688mm (66.6in)

Height: 1,416mm (55.7in)

Luggage capacity: 150–680 litres (5.29-24cu ft)

Top speed: 126mph

Acceleration, 0–60mph: 7.6sec

Fuel consumption, average: 40mpg

Price when new: £11,600

In profile, the new car exaggerated the original Mini in every direction but retained its stylistic flavour.

Did You Know?

The new MINI was launched in 2001 with a start price of £10,300 (the original cost £498 42 years earlier). Its wheels were exactly 50 per cent larger at 15in (against 10in), its engine had an almost 50 per cent larger capacity at 1,598cc (848cc) and its 89bhp power output was 160 per cent greater (34bhp).

Chrome accents tweaked nostalgic longings, and two-tone paintwork was a key feature.

▶ By the end of 2002,
the range consisted
of (left to right) One,
Cooper and Cooper S.

▶▶ MINI Cooper in
action – the new car won
widespread praise for its
handling, roadholding
and fun factor.

In 2003, the MINI took on the USA, promptly scooping the North American Car of the Year award.

This was an all-alloy engine all right, with a capacity of 1598cc, one boasting a 16-valve head too, but it was co-developed as the Tritec with Chrysler and would also be found in the Chrysler Neon. It was transversely-mounted and drove the front wheels like a 'proper' Mini.

The old car had only ever offered a four-speed manual gearbox or a conventional automatic transmission, but now there was either a five-speed manual or an electronic continuously-variable automatic; the latter featured a semi-automatic button shift control on the steering wheel. Of rubber suspension systems there was no trace, with MacPherson struts at the front and a multi-link rear axle. There were disc brakes front and back, with electronically-controlled stability and brake force application programmes as standard, and a drive-by-wire throttle. Traction control was optional. It was the first production car with a tyre defect indicator as part of a comprehensive safety package packed with airbags, along with optional run-flat tyres.

In January 2002 the MINI range was boosted – literally – by the addition of the high-performance Cooper S. Its lightning acceleration of 0.62mph in 7.5 seconds and 135mph top speed was down to a supercharged engine with 163bhp on tap. The supercharger fitment meant the battery had to be housed in the boot; hence there was no spare wheel, and run-flat tyres were standard. A six-speed manual transmission was included, together with a taut sports suspension package. It was on sale by June that year, and the following year was joined by the first ever diesel MINI, powered by a common-rail 1.4-litre

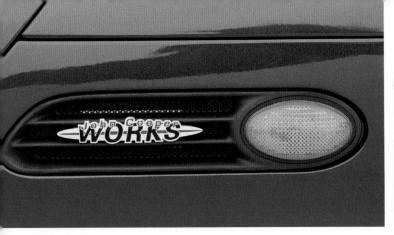

The authentic Cooper connection returned in 2003 with a range of high-performance models and additions.

Mike Cooper is a big boy now, and keeping the family garage and tuning businesses humming.

It's 25 August 2004 and the half-millionth MINI is about to drive into British motoring history.

Toyota turbodiesel. This was the MINI One D and its sparing fuel thirst allowed 58mph.

Cooper cars, moreover, could be filled with John Cooper Works tuning and styling packages, all endorsed by Cooper's son Mike (JC died in 2000) and his company. These were but one part of an enormous factory customisation and accessories programme that meant, along with the

Just 2,000 of these lightweight John Cooper Works GP Kit cars were built.

availability of two-tone paintwork, very few MINIs would end up identical.

Next up, in 2004, was the MINI Convertible with a power-operated fabric roof, glass rear window and, in a small tribute to Issigonis's thinking, a drop-down boot with external hinges that was a logical solution to accommodating the hood's folding mechanism. The roof section above the driver and front passenger could also be slid back electrically for a coupe-de-ville feel. And it was offered with every engine except the diesel. Some 163,000 of them were sold in the following four years.

⋀ John Cooper Works GP Kit even ditched the rear seat in an effort to trim speed-sapping lard.

⋀ ⋀ BMW unveiled this hydrogen-powered MINI Cooper in 2001; a decade on and it remains a prototype.

➤ The first ever diesel Mini, the One D, arrived in 2003, bringing 58mpg economy with it.

Did You Know?
The 2004 MINI XXL was not the first Mini six-wheeler: the 1970 Scamp and 1979 Interstyl Hustler were both Mini-based kit cars available in six-wheeler versions that could be built at home.

The MINI Convertible of 2004 (this is a One) was dedicated to wind-in-the-hair exhilaration.

▶ The MINI marketing people never miss a trick: this Mandarin Duck luggage set was tailor-made for the Convertible's small boot.

▶▶ The MINI MkII received a top-of-the-form five-star safety rating in Euro NCAP crash tests in 2007.

A limited edition that has real significance is the Cooper S John Cooper Works GP Kit of 2006. Only 2,000 were hand-finished by Bertone in Italy, with 459 finding British owners. It was a stripped-out semi-racer for the road, its weight-saving attributes including no rear seats, rear wash/wipe or air-con, and minimal sound-deadening material. It was given a stiffened, reinforced body, an aerodynamic undercarriage, and a carbon-fibre rear spoiler. It's a dead cert as a future collector's car.

That the car was a massive success was not in doubt. The 500,000th new MINI – a silver Cooper S – was built in August 2004, 37 months since hitting showrooms. Its sales pace was fractionally ahead of the original Mini's; records reveal 509,572 had been sold by the end of 1962 – three years and four months later.

109

▲ Freshly-painted MINI bodies at Plant Oxford, where BMW spent £100 million on enlarging the paintshop and assembly line for the new soft-top models.

➤ Both Hatch and Convertible are built up in rotary slings on the Oxford production line.

One wacky way to promote the new MINI was to turn it into a six-wheeled stretch limo. Oh, and then add a swimming pool.

With Splitdoor at the back and Clubdoor at the side, the Clubman opened up the MINI's practical side.

◀ With MINI, you can have everything with anything; this is the Clubman in full-on John Cooper Works glory. It'll do 148mph!

▼ The interior of the MkII Convertible can be turned over from hedonism to handiness with a few deft clicks.

FACTS & DATA: MINI COOPER D CLUBMAN

On sale: 2007–11

Engine capacity: 1598cc (turbodiesel)

Engine bore/stroke: 78/83.6mm

Engine power output: 110bhp at 4,000rpm

Fuel system: fuel-injection

Bodystyle: five-door, four-seater estate

Wheelbase: 2,547mm (100.3in)

Length: 3,961mm (155.9in)

Width: 1,683mm (66.3in)

Height: 1,426mm (56.1in)

Luggage capacity: 260–930 litres (9.1-32.8cu ft)

Top speed: 122mph

Acceleration, 0–60mph: 9.1sec

Fuel consumption, average: 43.9mpg

Price when new: £14,235

The Cooper proved the biggest selling variant thus far, with 250,000 shifted. The two cars' starkest showroom performance was in exports. Some 284,000 of the half-million-plus-a-few 1959–62 original Minis were sold abroad, but BMW had already shipped 375,000 of the half-million new ones. This included cars to the USA, where the original Mini barely figured. These were all Cooper or Cooper S models, as the One was deemed not powerful enough to support standard air conditioning without seriously blunted performance.

Typically these days, the car industry has a replacement cycle of about five years that would have been anathema to Alec Issigonis, whose Morris Minor was on sale for 23 years and Mini for an incredible 41. So it is that the new MINI was replaced by, ahem, a 'new' MINI in 2006. Still, you would have been hard-pressed to tell the difference even quite close up when it arrived in November 2006. It was comprehensively re-engineered inside and out to the extent that every single panel was new. The raised nose now had headlights in the conventional position anchored into the body structure, rather than as part of the previous 'clamshell' bonnet that had seen virtually the entire front of the car lift to reveal the power unit inside.

The car was even safer. Six airbags, three-point seatbelts throughout, ISOFIX child fastenings at the rear, and central safety electronics to manage the car's restraint system were all features. The state-of-the-art chassis helped it win the coveted five-star rating in Euro NCAP crash tests.

◁ All MINI Convertibles – this is a MkII – have power-operated hoods, the front portion of which can slide back like a sunroof.

Did You Know?
By 2006, the UK was still the biggest market for the MINI, while America and Germany were second and third respectively.

≫ *MINI sales chief Ian Robertson shows the electric MINI E to former Labour government figures Gordon Brown, Peter Mandelson and Geoff Hoon.*

≫≫ *The 1.4-litre MINI First, a new basic model in 2009, sought to reaffirm the car as ideal for those on a relatively tight budget; it cost £10,950.*

In came a brand new 1.6-litre petrol engine for the Cooper, with fully variable valve control for seamless delivery of its 120bhp of power, designed in partnership with Peugeot and manufactured by BMW at Hams Hall (Tritecs had been imported from Brazil). Both thriftier and more responsive, the new motor was loaded with BMW's latest technology, including Brake Energy Regeneration, Auto Start/Stop, a gearshift point indicator, a volume-flow-controlled oil pump, and an on-demand coolant pump. The One received a 1397cc engine, offering a milder 95bhp (or 75bhp in an economy edition – only 109mph possible, but the 53mpg economy was the big deal here). There was a fuel-conserving yet lively 1.6 turbodiesel too, with a phenomenal 72mpg on offer, plus a CO_2 emissions rating of a mere 104g per km. Even more pertinent to the driver was electric power steering and a six-speed manual gearbox in every model, no matter how lowly, and with a steering wheel paddle shift option.

The virtually all-new MINI Cooper S switched to turbocharging to get its zest, which was now engine power of 175bhp at 5,500rpm and torque of 177lb/ft anywhere between 1,600 and 5,000rpm, with an Overboost function briefly increasing torque to 192lb/ft when called for. It was now a 140mph machine that could sprint to 62mph from a standstill in just 7.1 seconds. Yet it could still attain 30mpg.

The new MINI Clubman made its much-anticipated debut at the 2007 Frankfurt Motor Show. There was no actual link to the 1969–80 Clubman bar the name, but this was the first estate car since the original

The new, five-door MINI Countryman is a 'crossover' car that can be had with all-wheel drive.

Clubman-fronted HL was quietly dropped in 1982. In one key aspect, the 24cm-longer Clubman really did evoke the old Travellers and Countrymans of the 1960s; instead of the tailgate of other shooting brake-type cars, it had twin rear doors, each hinged at the side, and swinging open to take the corners of the car, but not the rear lights, with them. To maximise this novelty, BMW decided to baptise the feature as Splitdoor. It had another moniker for the ingenious rear-hinged side passenger door (on the left side of the car as you look at it from the front): Clubdoor. Oh, dear. Still, at least it made access to the roomier rear bench seat easier, despite being on the wrong side of the car for stopping on the roadside, maybe outside a school, in Britain.

The practical nature of the Clubman didn't stop it being available with John Cooper Works performance upgrades, just like the standard Hatch (they call this a Hardtop in the US and Australia) and the new-model Convertible that arrived in 2008.

These are based, loosely, on the MINI Challenge race series cars, which means an engine and 'twin-scroll' turbocharger tuned and reinforced to give 211bhp and, thanks to increased charge pressure, maximum torque of 260Nm (192lb/ft) at anything from 1,850rpm upwards and a momentary boost to 280Nm (206lb/ft) when accelerating between 1,950–5,500rpm. Astonishingly responsive to right-foot urges, then, and all with an appropriately adapted six-speed gearbox and 17in alloy wheels. Such Hatches and Clubmans need just 6.8 seconds to hit 62mph, and can do 148mph; Convertibles slightly less on both counts.

◀ *Countryman accommodation is very much family-orientated, but with familiar MINI touches.*

The MINI's importance to the health of the British motor industry, despite its ultimate ownership in Munich, is crucial. When the decision was taken, in 2000, to make the old Morris Motors plant at Cowley on the outskirts of Oxford the bedrock of the new MINI enterprise, BMW was updating a factory that had already had £280 million invested in its bodyshop and assembly lines in 1996/7, while a new paintshop was dwarfed only by the Millennium Dome in terms of contemporary British construction projects. For the arrival of the MINI, BMW splashed another £230 million modernising the 85-year-old former domain of the Morris Minor ready for the first car to roll off the production line in July 2001. This included installing 229 robots and an electronic documentation system that sees cars through from bare metal to

◀ This MINI Coupé
Concept was unveiled
in 2009; a version of it
is scheduled to enter
production in 2011.

finished article; this is especially important as each car is specified by the customer and dealer, including all options and finishes, before its manufacture commences. There is no such thing as a MINI 'from stock'.

The entire process was overhauled yet again in 2005 for the MkII. A further £100 million bought an additional paintshop and an enlarged body assembly department to take annual capacity to 240,000 cars. The start of MkII production in autumn 2006 also pressed the button on the so-called MINI Production Triangle. Body pressings were stamped in Swindon while engines were now manufactured in Hams Hall, with all components united at Plant Oxford to be turned into new MINIs. British content on the MkII among each car's 2,000 components leapt from 40 to 60 per cent, and the workforce numbered 1,000 at Swindon, 1,000 at Hams Hall and 3,700 at Oxford. The only time when the three teams haven't contributed entirely to British-built MINIs was on the MINI E; 500 'glider' examples of this electric car were completed at Oxford without petrol engines, their electric powertrain being installed in Munich before they were assigned to field tests in the hands of lessees. Possible mass production is pencilled in for 2013.

In January 2010, the MINI Countryman arrived, and caused instant consternation among marque aficionados. On the upside, here was a larger, taller car with its five seats and five doors making it the first MINI that could properly be called a family car. The availability of all-wheel drive on Cooper and Cooper S variants also elevated it to 'crossover' status, with the grip and

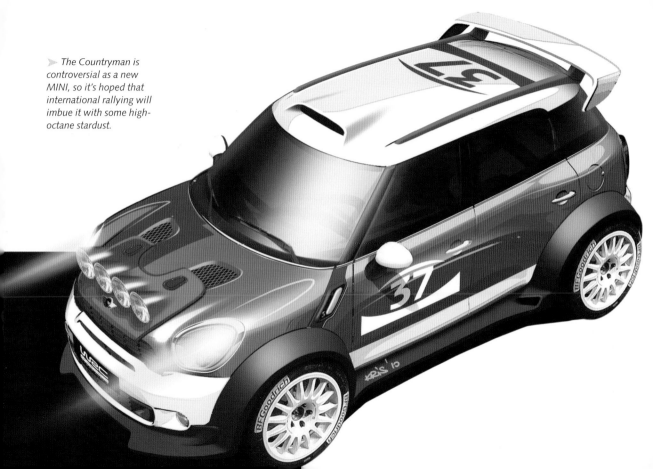

The Countryman is controversial as a new MINI, so it's hoped that international rallying will imbue it with some high-octane stardust.

stature to make it a compact alternative to a Land Rover Freelander in the desolate wastes of tree-lined suburbia. The regular MINI's engine range was carried over and the family resemblance was maintained by using huge wheels and black wheelarches to mask the extra bulk.

And the downside? Well, early rumours that it was nothing but a thinly-disguised BMW X1 were soon dispelled. Not true; they're entirely different. The MINI engines are transverse while the BMW's are in-line. It isn't built in Leipzig like the X1 but it is assembled in Austria, and so becomes the first Mini/MINI to be sourced entirely outside the UK from the start.

Nonetheless, in the spirit of a company renowned for the care and passion it lavishes on everything it does, BMW has a plan to make the Countryman itself an icon. In July 2010 it announced the chubby saloon would be going rallying in the spirit of the original Mini's glory days of the 1960s. The full assault, orchestrated by those former Subaru miracle workers at Britain's Prodrive is set for 2012. Whatever the outcome, it will be more Mini history in the making.

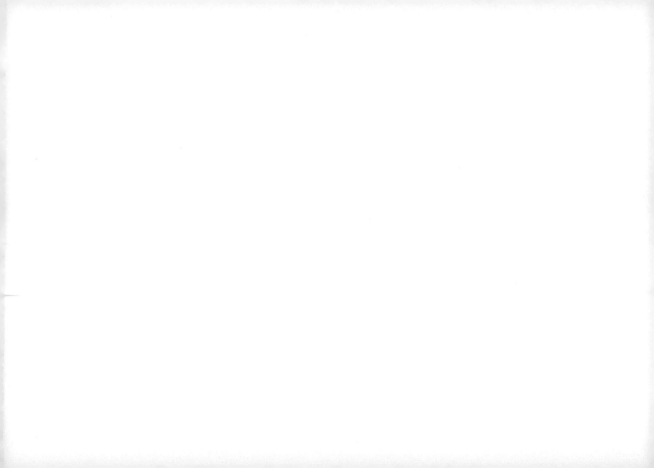